This Book Belongs to

____

____

____

A is for Avocado

Trace the letters with a pencil. Then practice writing the letters on the lines

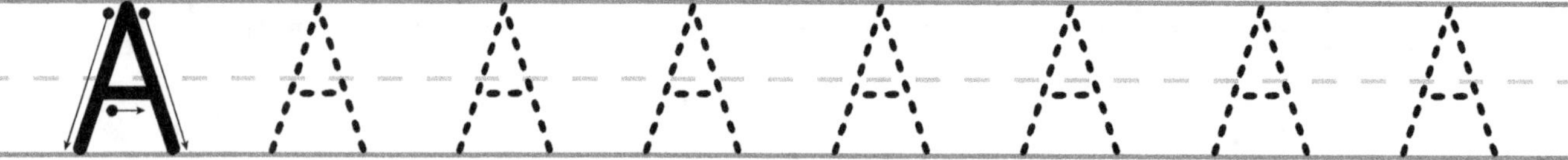

a a a a a a a a

PRACTICE WORKSHEET

A A A A A A A A

a a a a a a a a a

A A A A A A A A

a a a a a a a a a

B is for Beans

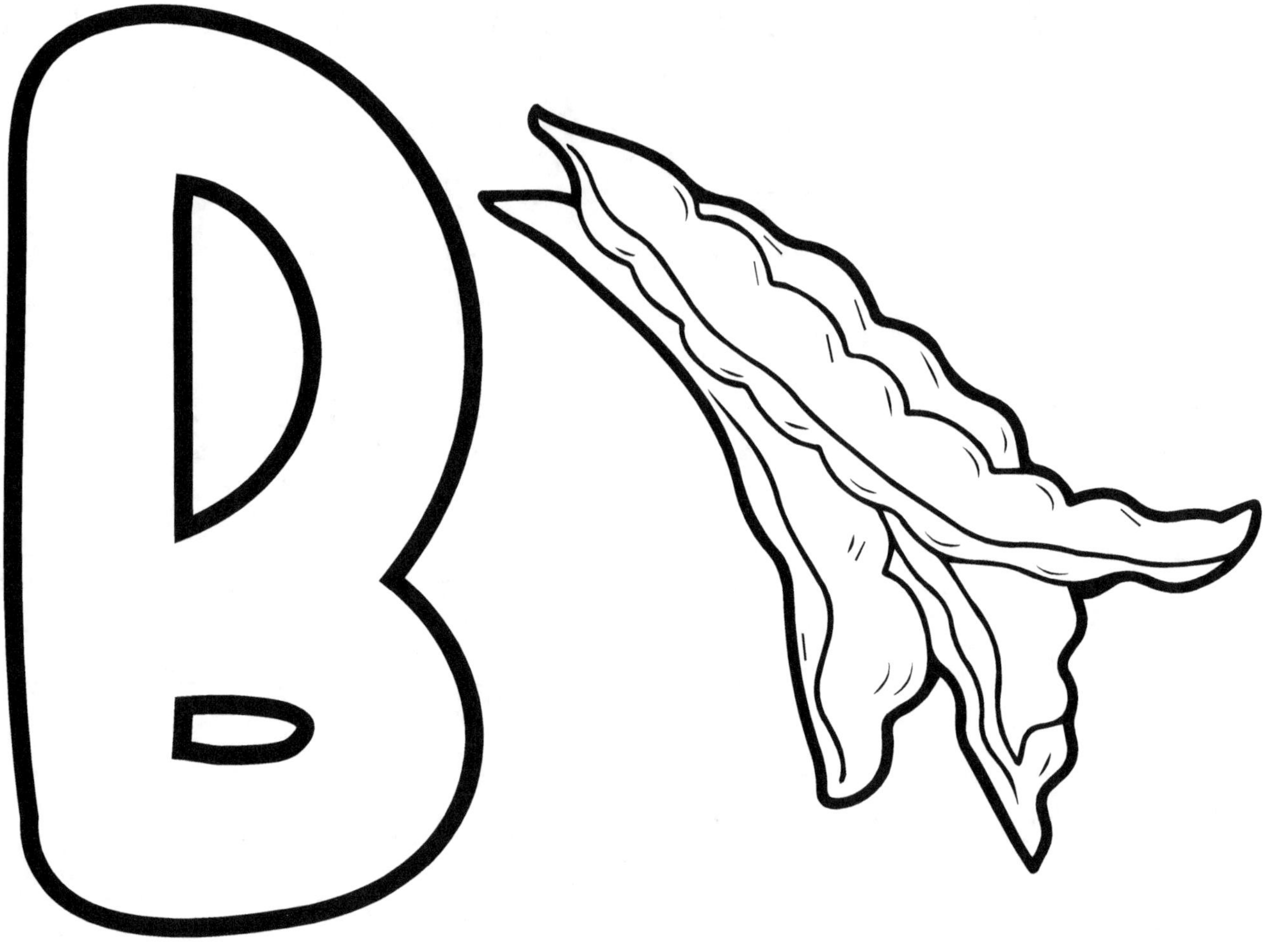

Trace the letters with a pencil. Then practice writing the letters on the lines

B B B B B B B B

b b b b b b b b

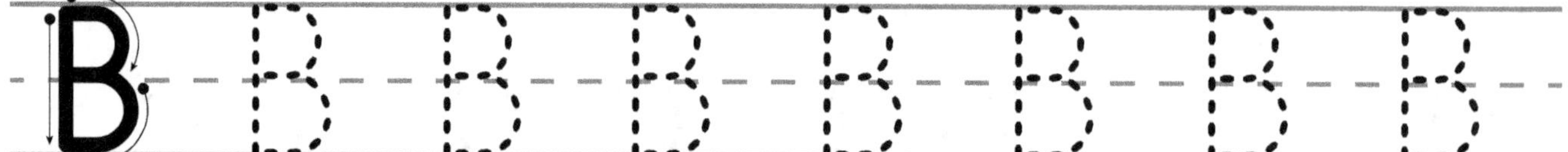

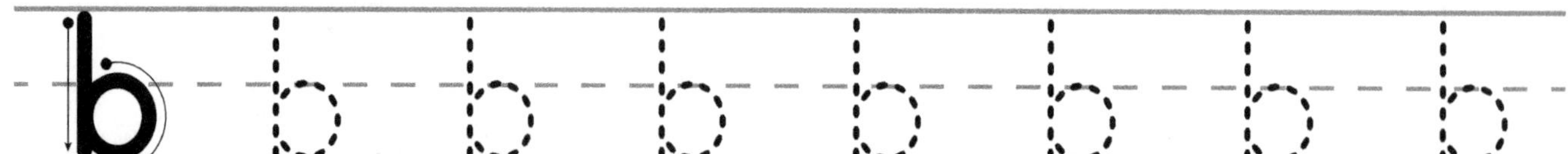

PRACTICE WORKSHEET

B B B B B B B B

b b b b b b b b

B B B B B B B B

b b b b b b b b

C is for Coconut

Trace the letters with a pencil. Then practice writing the letters on the lines

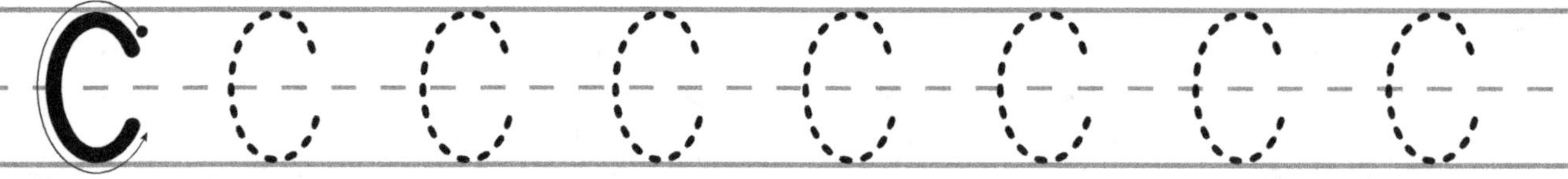

PRACTICE WORKSHEET

D is for Donut

Trace the letters with a pencil. Then practice writing the letters on the lines

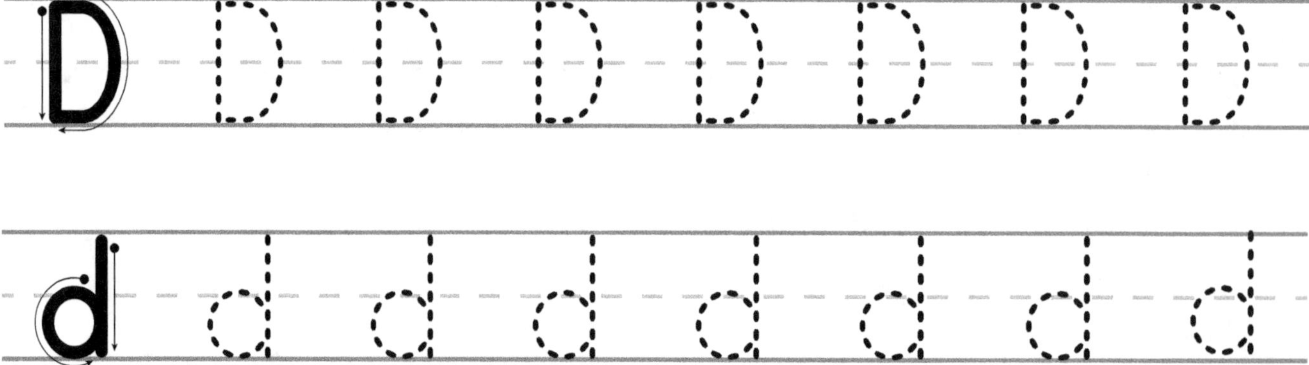

PRACTICE WORKSHEET

D D D D D D D D

d d d d d d d d

D D D D D D D D

d d d d d d d d

E is for Eggplant

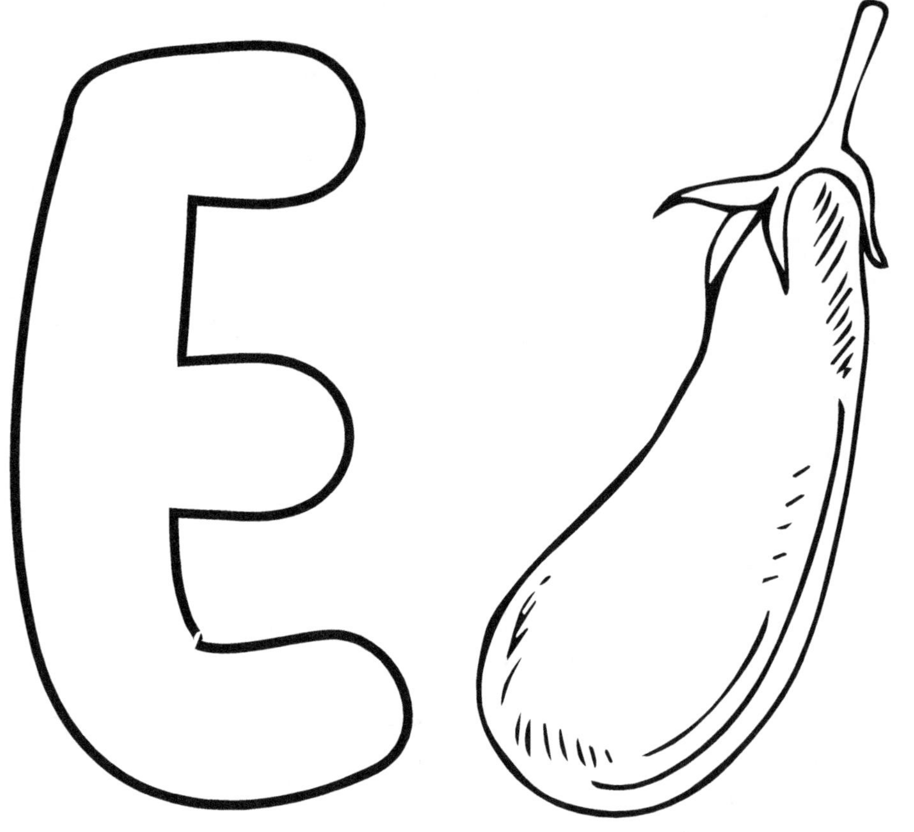

Trace the letters with a pencil. Then practice writing the letters on the lines

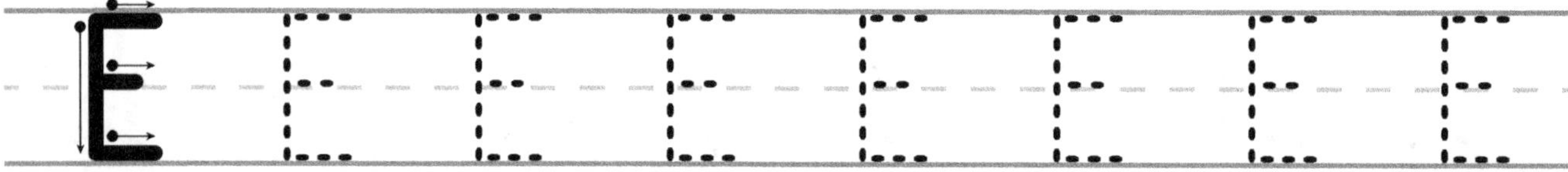

PRACTICE WORKSHEET

E E E E E E E E

e e e e e e e e

E E E E E E E E

e e e e e e e e

F is For French Toast

Trace the letters with a pencil. Then practice writing the letters on the lines

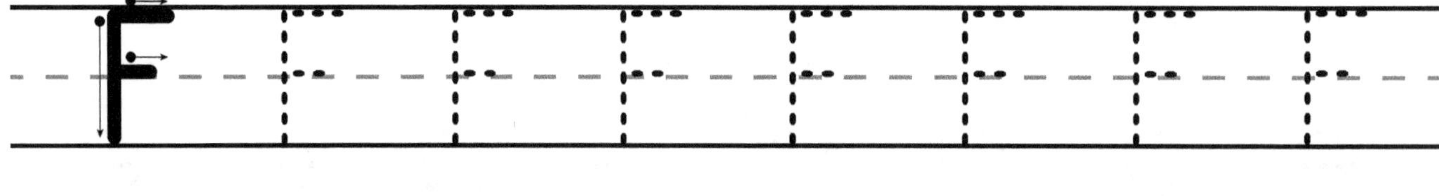

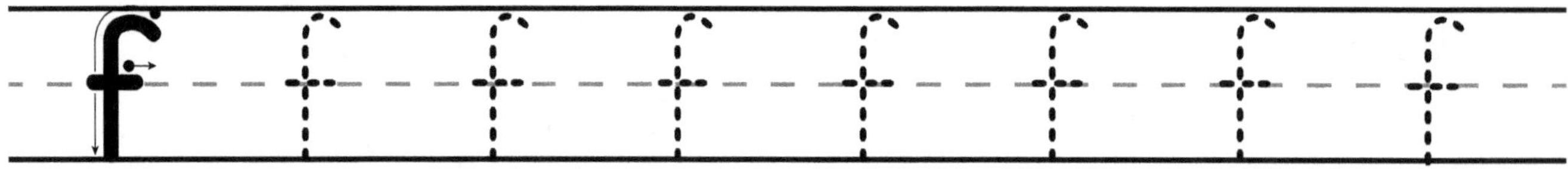

PRACTICE WORKSHEET

F F F F F F F F

f f f f f f f f

F F F F F F F F

f f f f f f f f

G is For Garlic

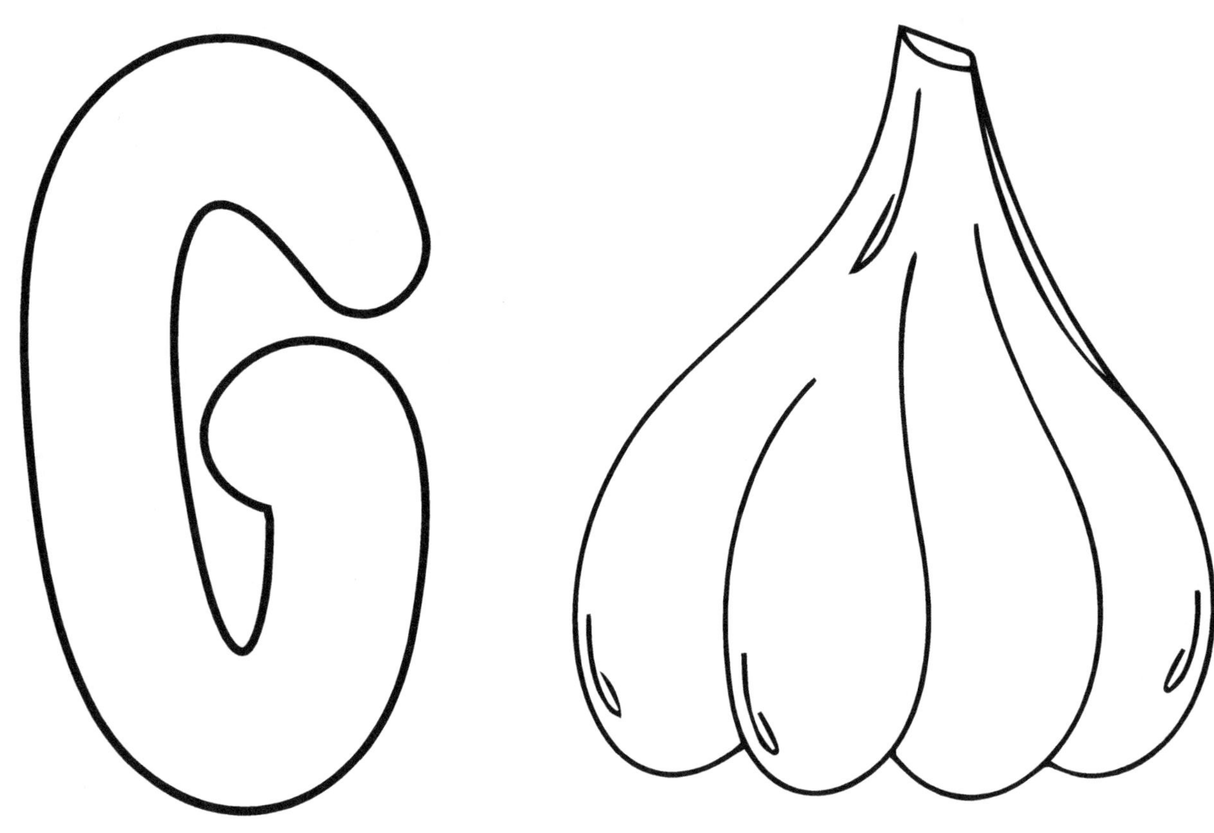

Trace the letters with a pencil. Then practice writing the letters on the lines

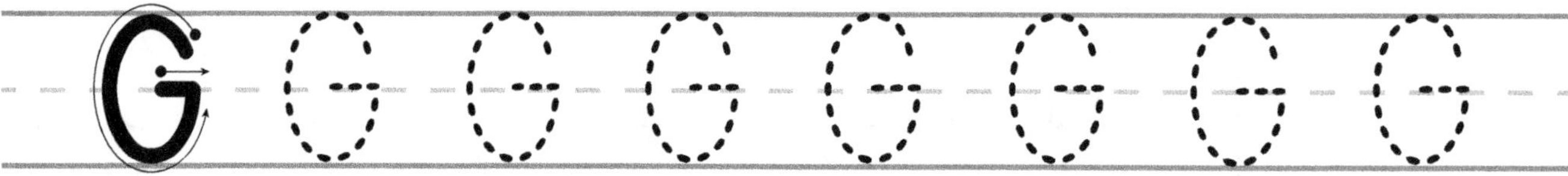

g g g g g g g g

PRACTICE WORKSHEET

H is For Hamburger

Trace the letters with a pencil. Then practice writing the letters on the lines

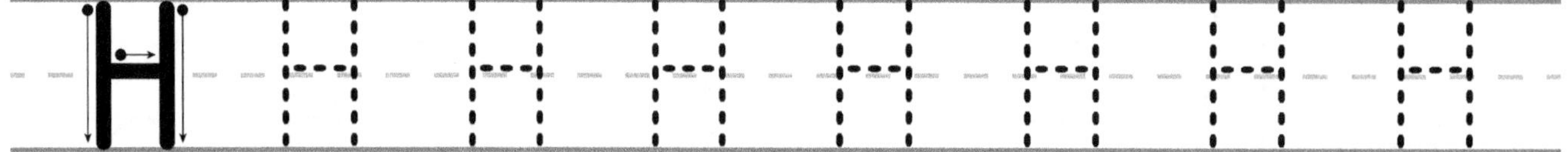

PRACTICE WORKSHEET

H H H H H H H H

h h h h h h h h

H H H H H H H H

h h h h h h h h

I is for Ice Cream

Trace the letters with a pencil. Then practice writing the letters on the lines

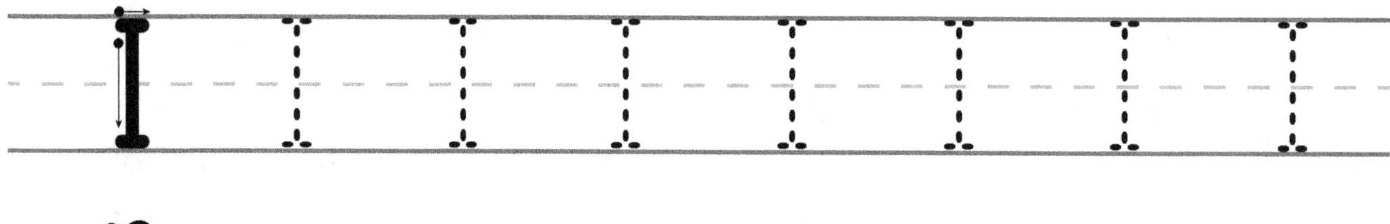

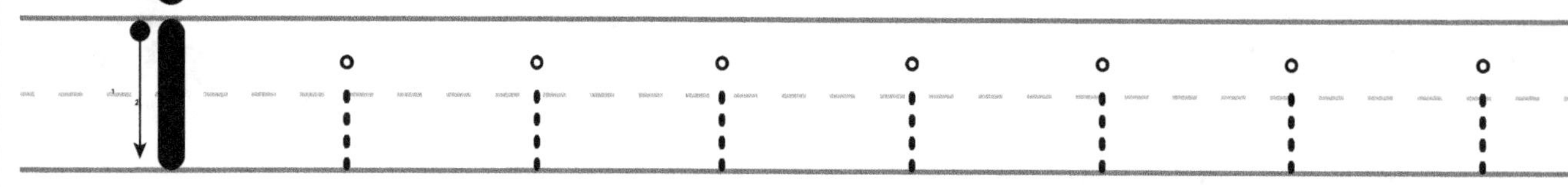

PRACTICE WORKSHEET

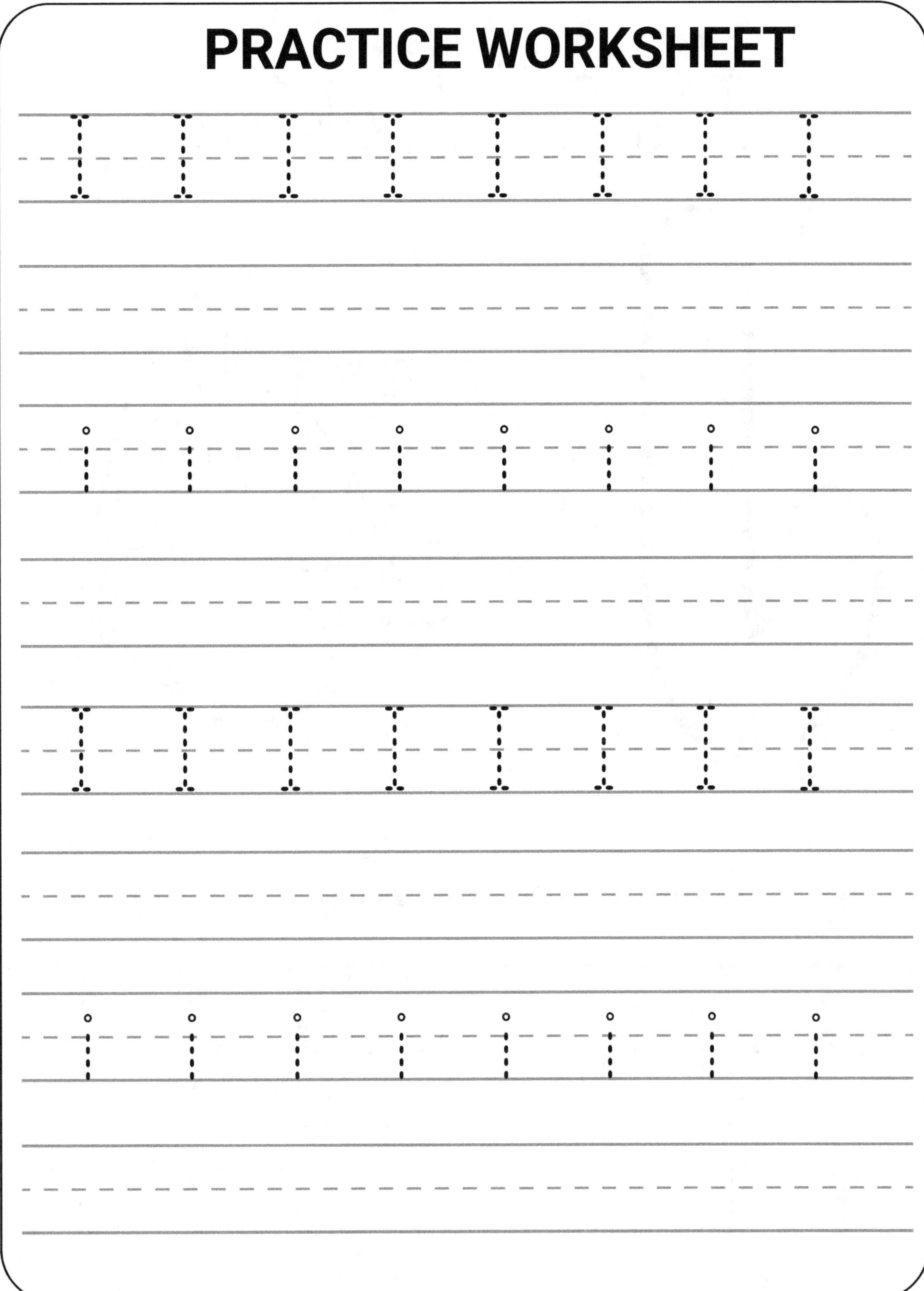

J is for Jackfruit

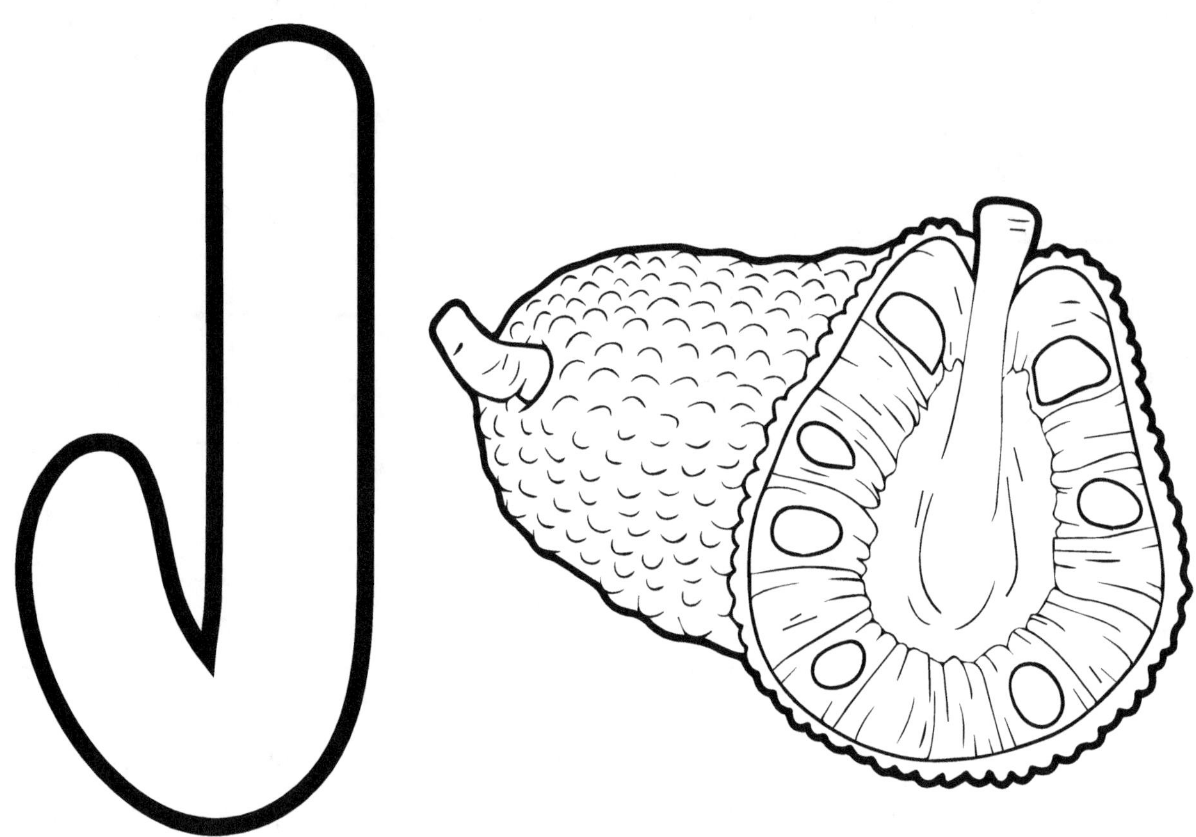

Trace the letters with a pencil. Then practice writing the letters on the lines

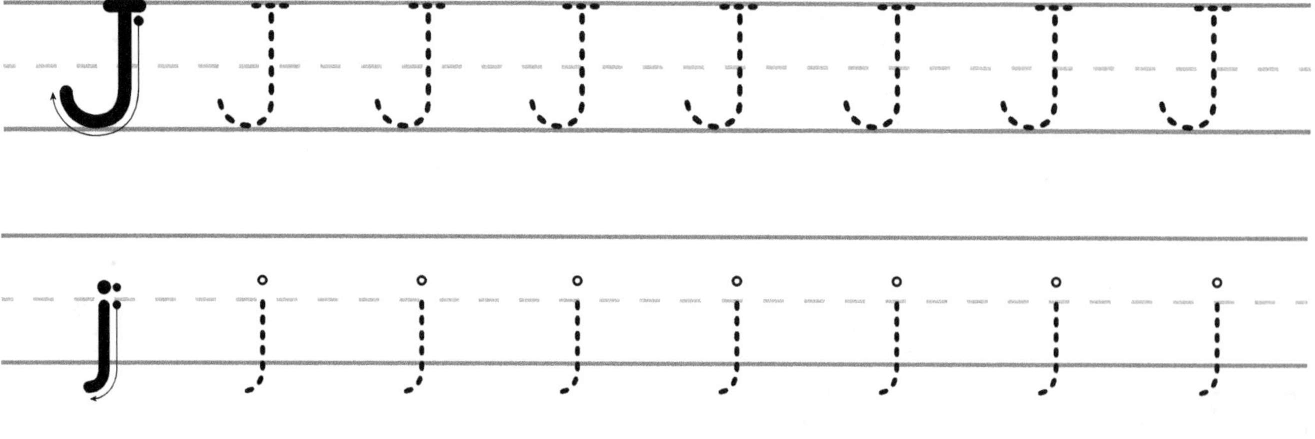

PRACTICE WORKSHEET

J J J J J J J J

j j j j j j j j

J J J J J J J J

j j j j j j j j

K is for Kale

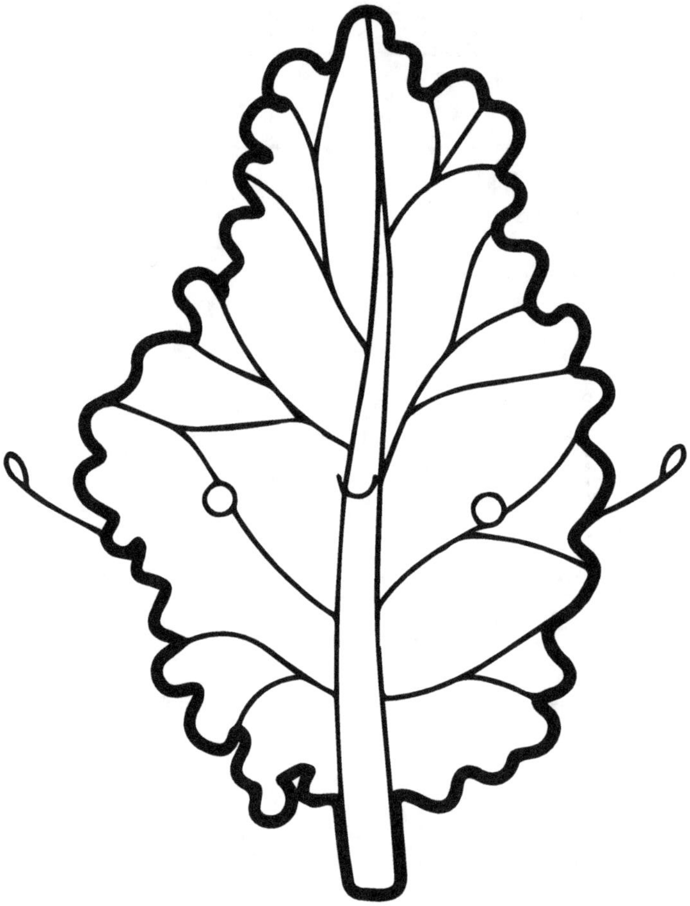

Trace the letters with a pencil. Then practice writing the letters on the lines

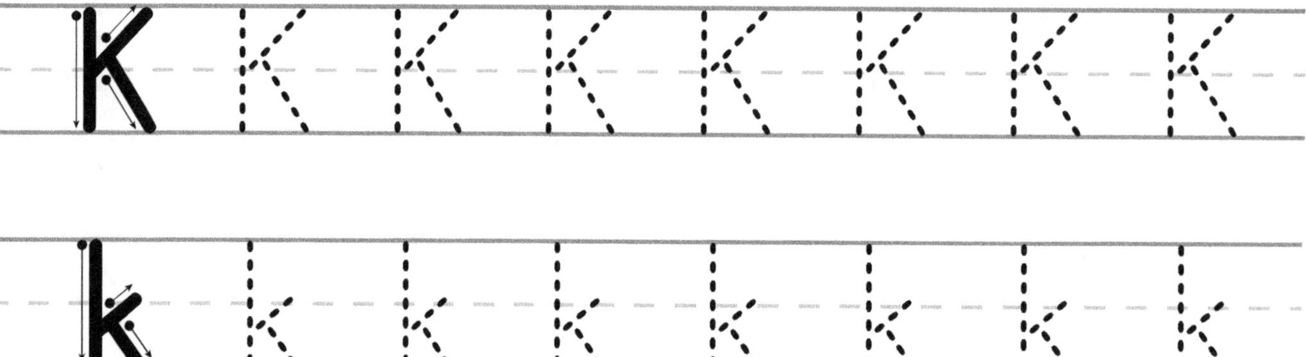

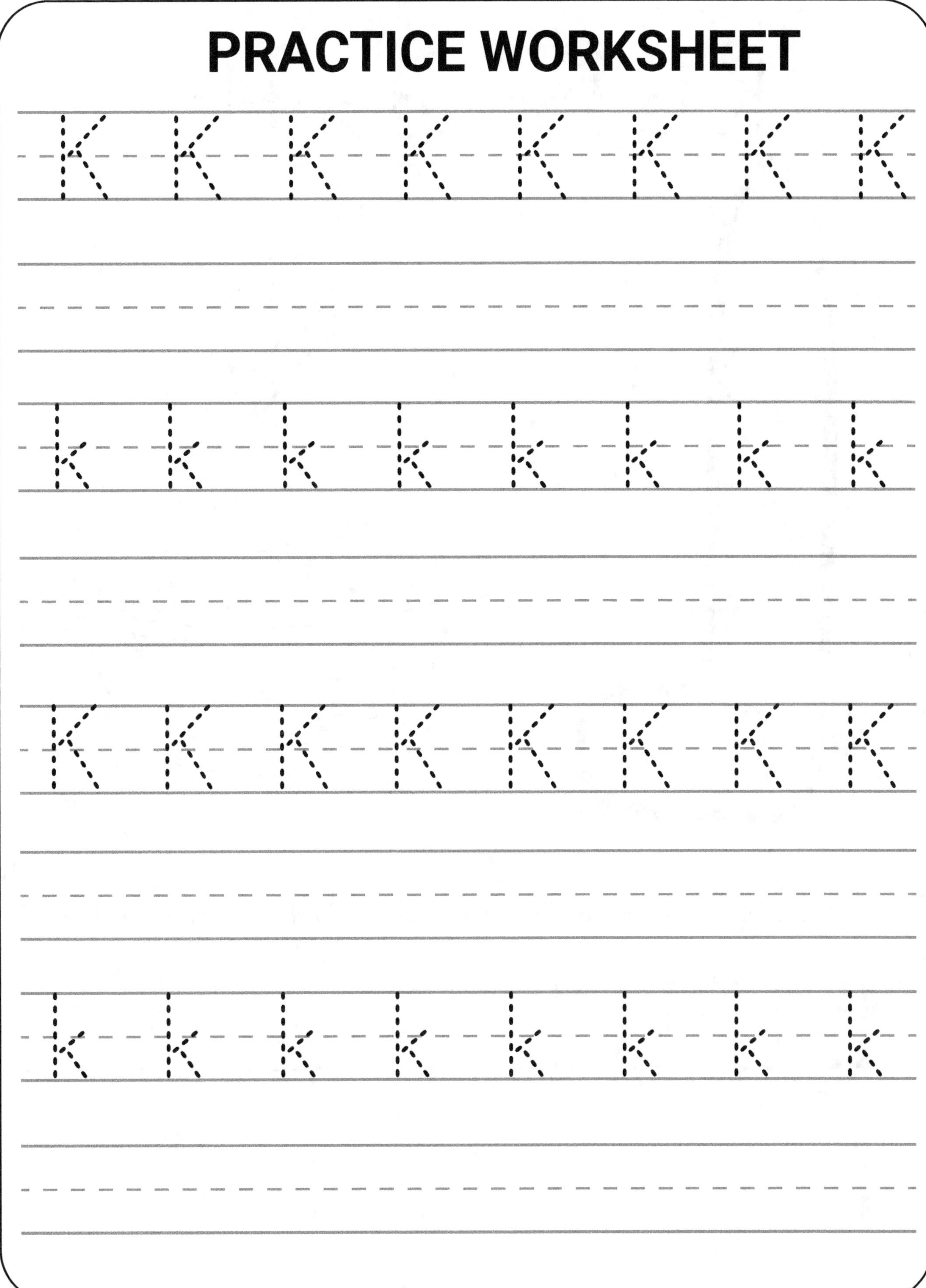
PRACTICE WORKSHEET
K K K K K K K K
k k k k k k k k
K K K K K K K K
k k k k k k k k

K is for Leantils

Trace the letters with a pencil. Then practice writing the letters on the lines

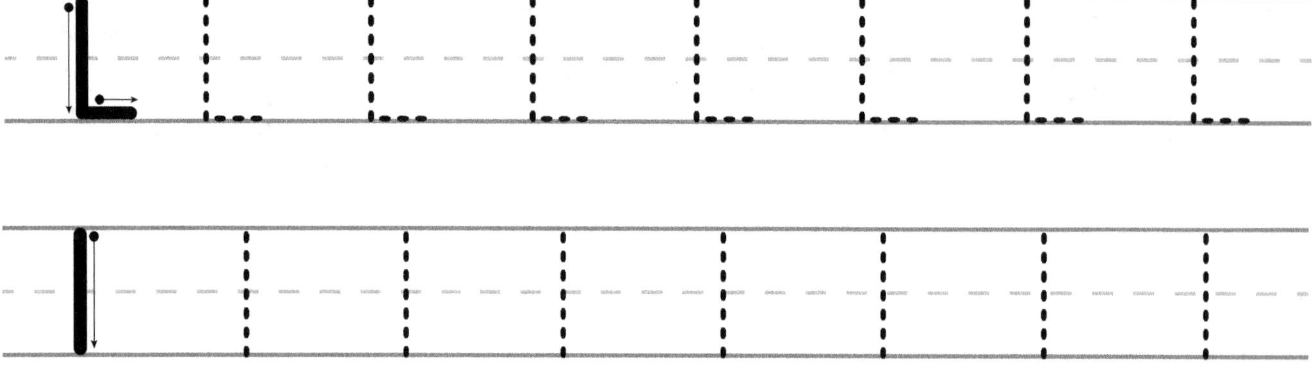

PRACTICE WORKSHEET

M is for Mushrooms

Trace the letters with a pencil. Then practice writing the letters on the lines

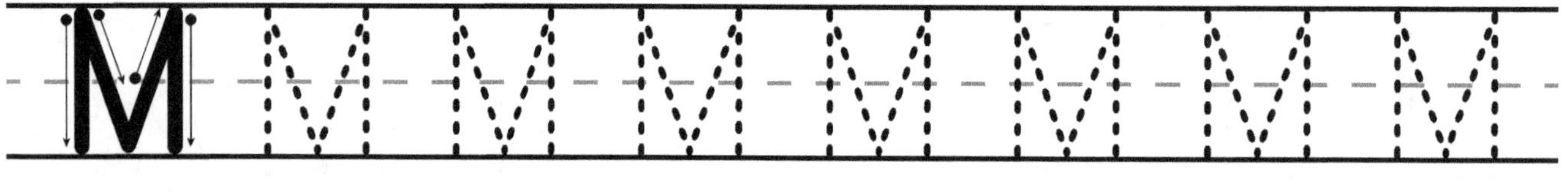

PRACTICE WORKSHEET

N is for Noodle

Trace the letters with a pencil. Then practice writing the letters on the lines

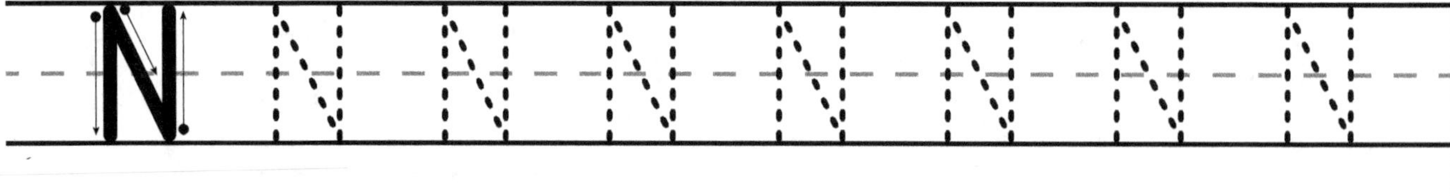

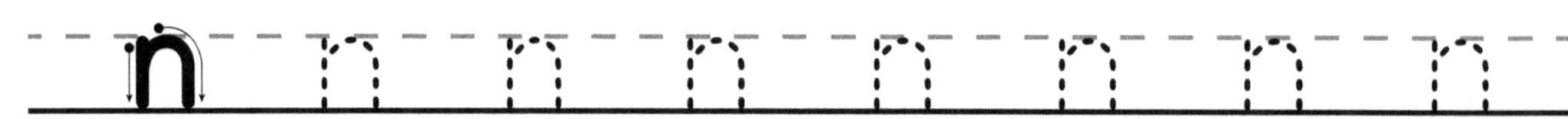

PRACTICE WORKSHEET

O is for Olives

Trace the letters with a pencil. Then practice writing the letters on the lines

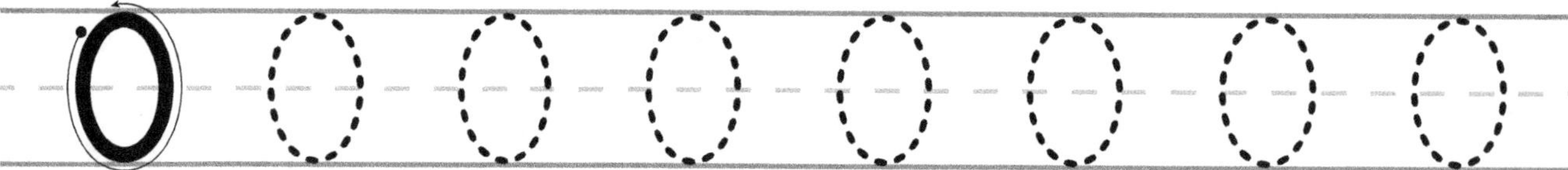

PRACTICE WORKSHEET

P is for Pastrami

P

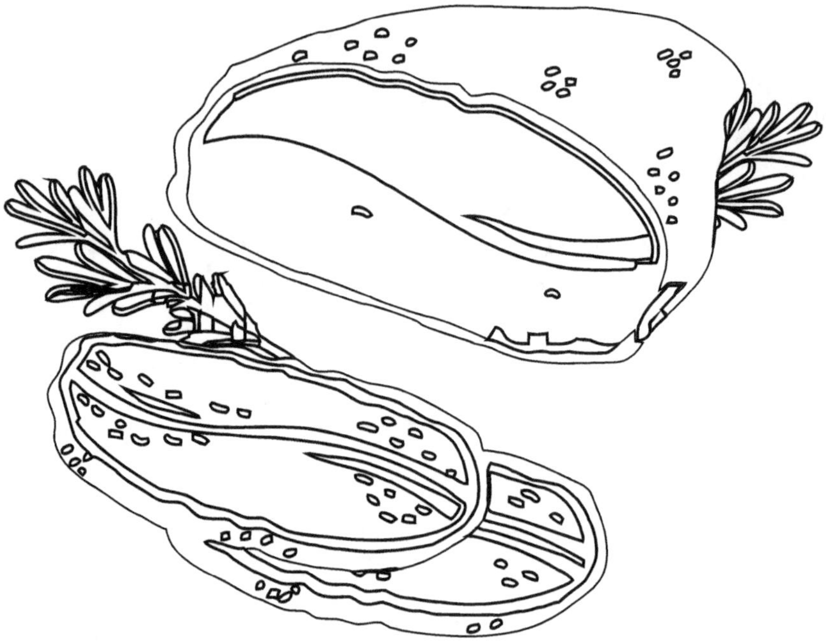

Trace the letters with a pencil. Then practice writing the letters on the lines

P P P P P P P P

p p p p p p p p

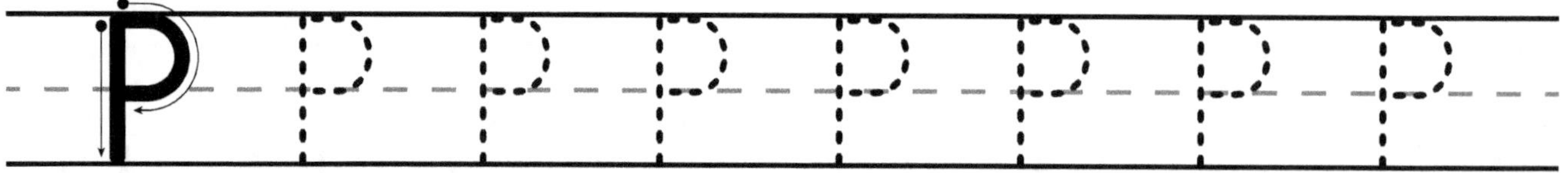

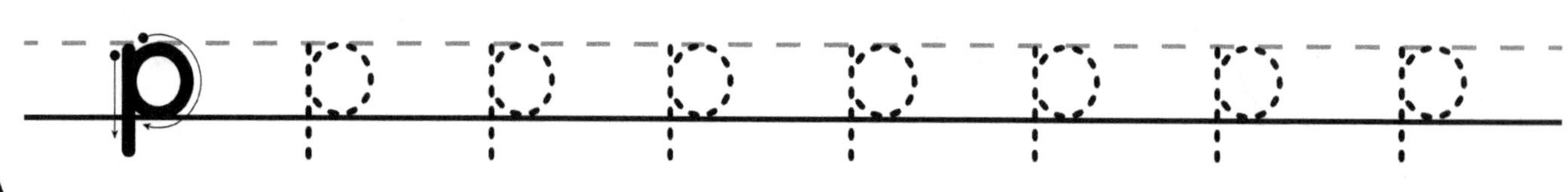

PRACTICE WORKSHEET

P P P P P P P P

p p p p p p p p

P P P P P P P P

p p p p p p p p

Q is for Quinoa

Trace the letters with a pencil. Then practice writing the letters on the lines

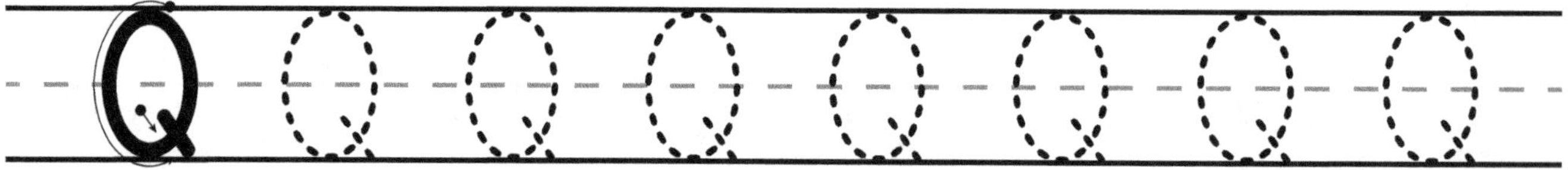

PRACTICE WORKSHEET

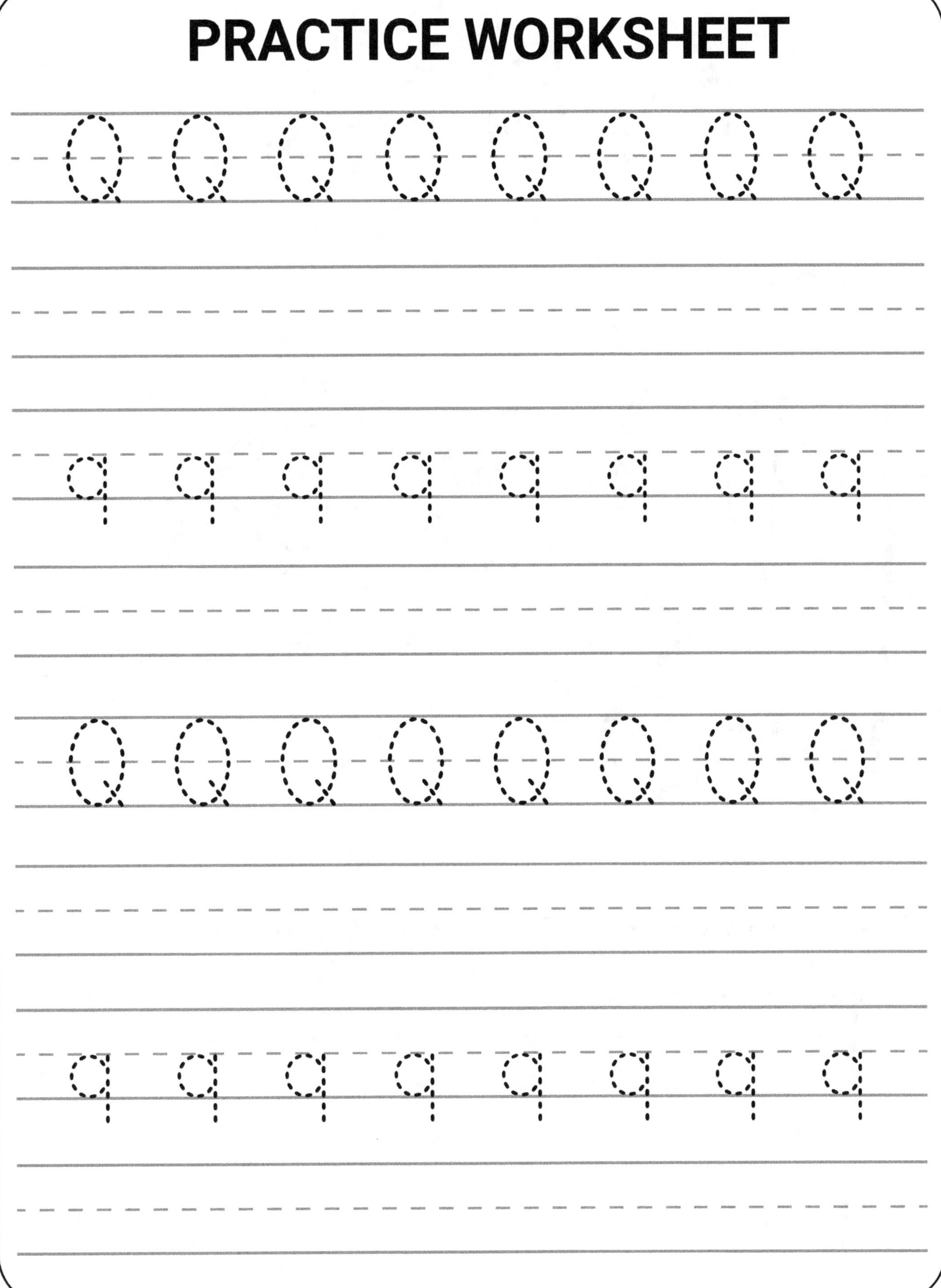

R is for Raisin

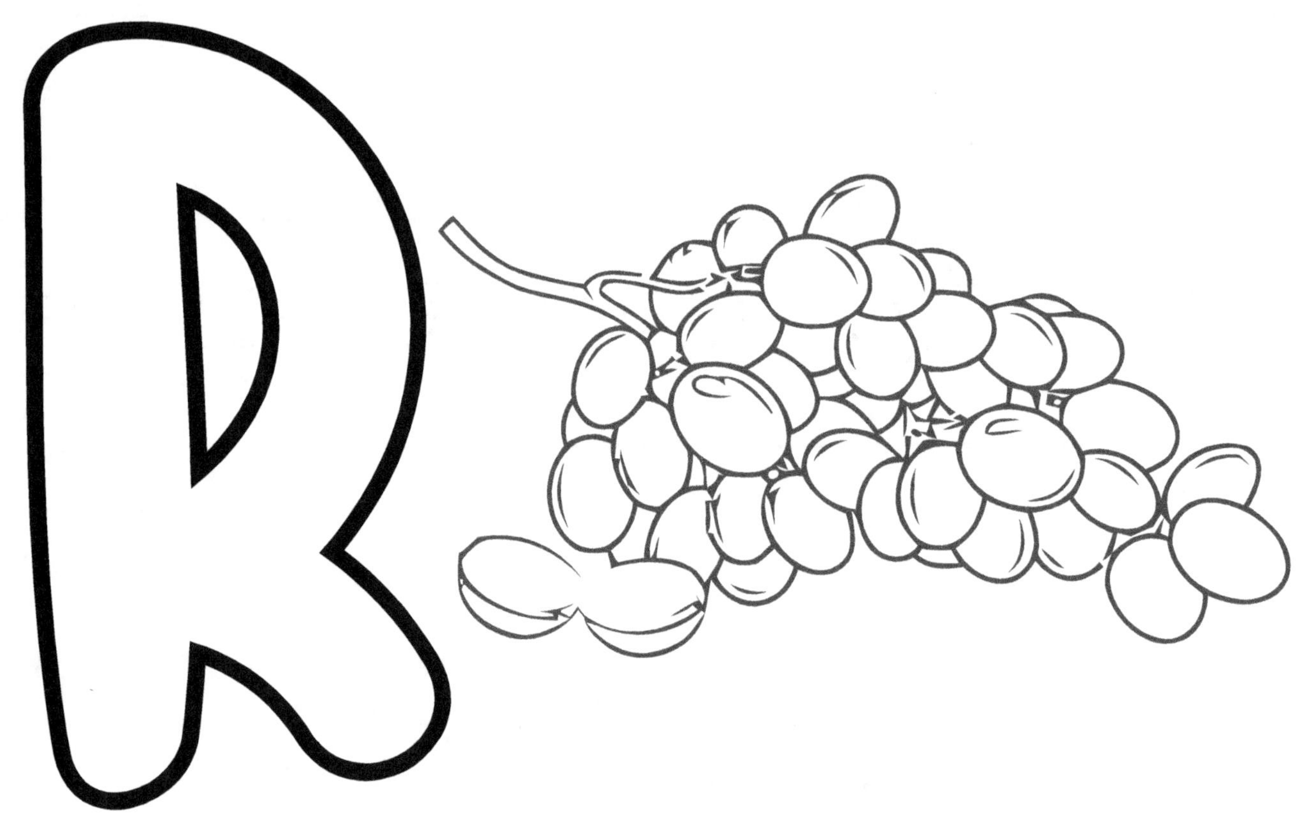

Trace the letters with a pencil. Then practice writing the letters on the lines

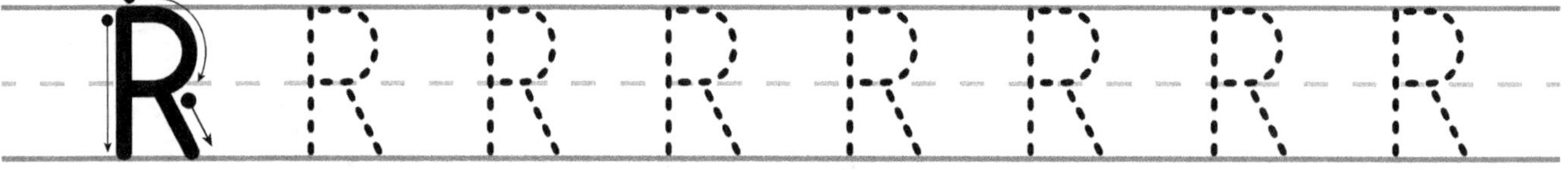

r r r r r r r r

PRACTICE WORKSHEET

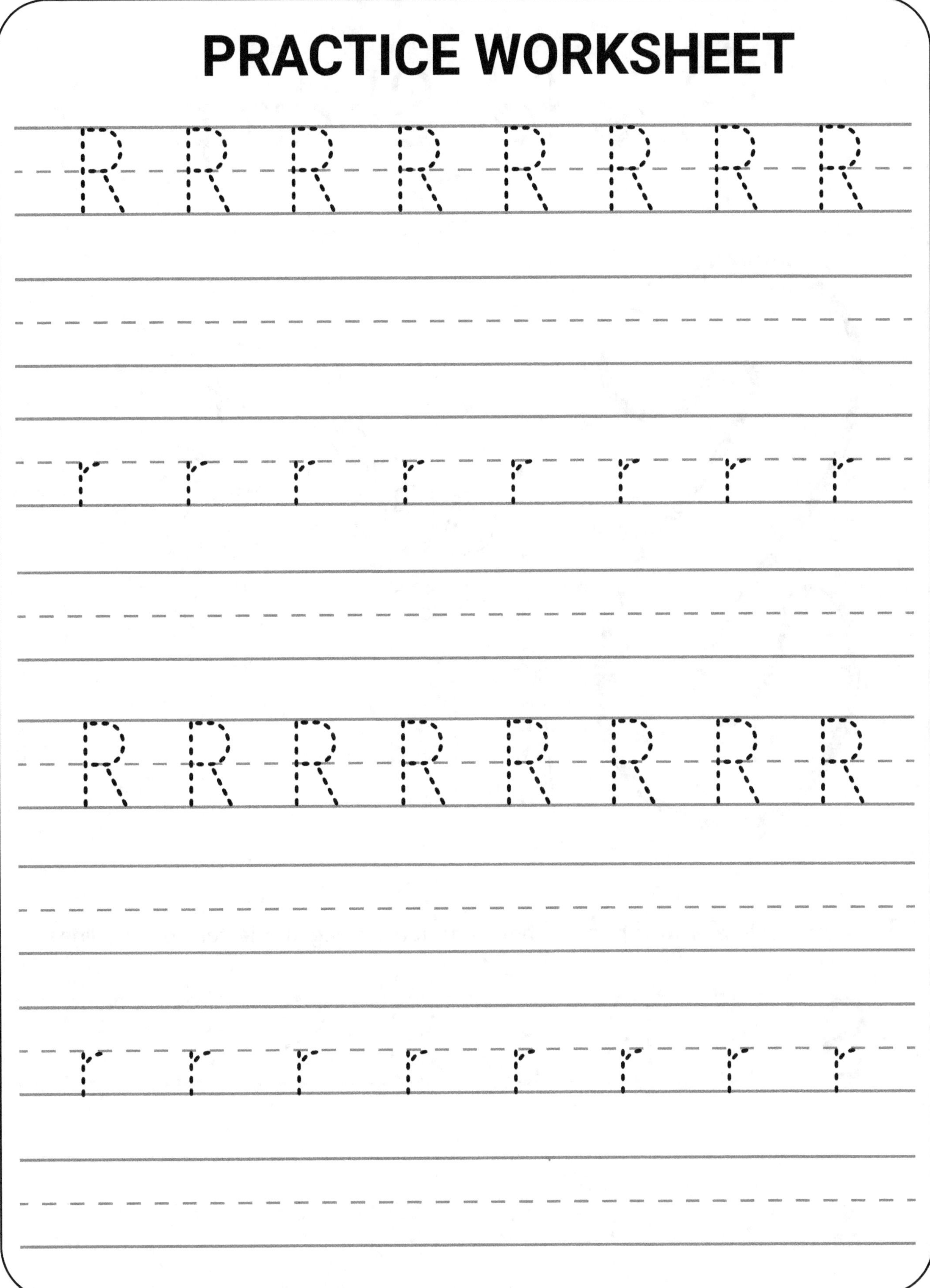

S is for Shrimp

1

S

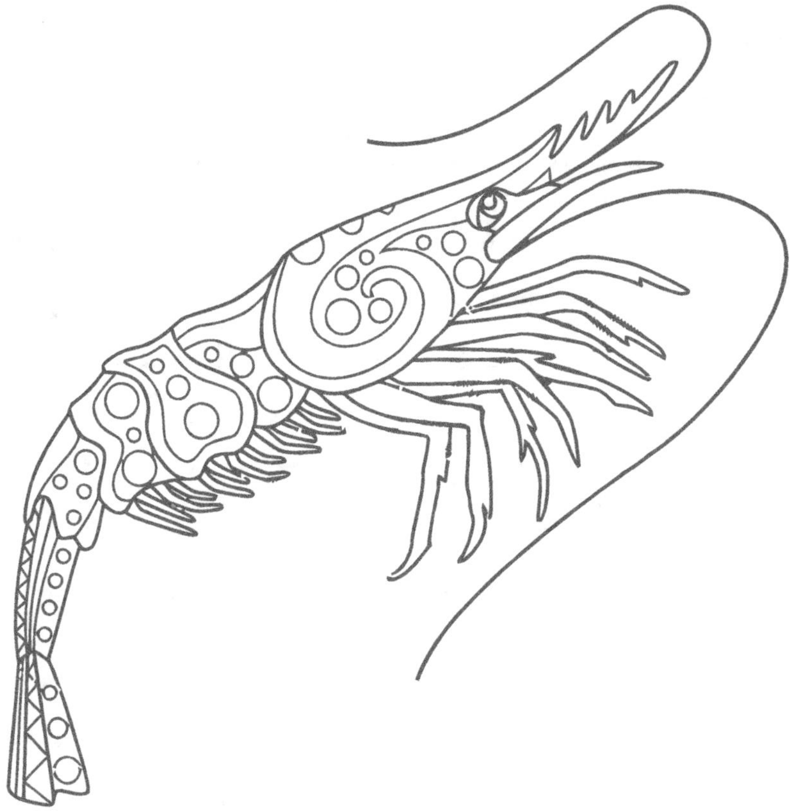

Trace the letters with a pencil. Then practice writing the letters on the lines

S S S S S S S S

s s s s s s s s

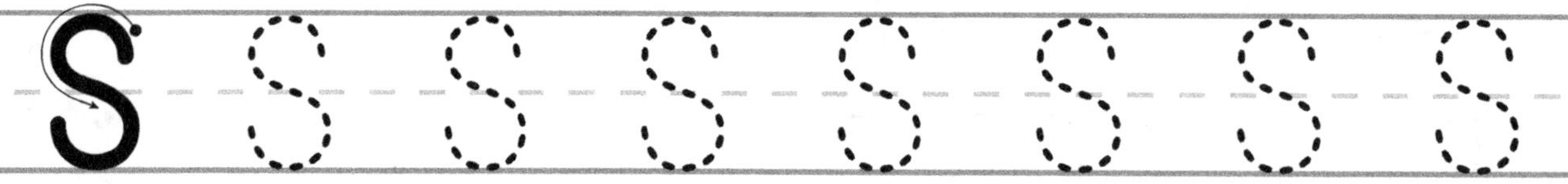

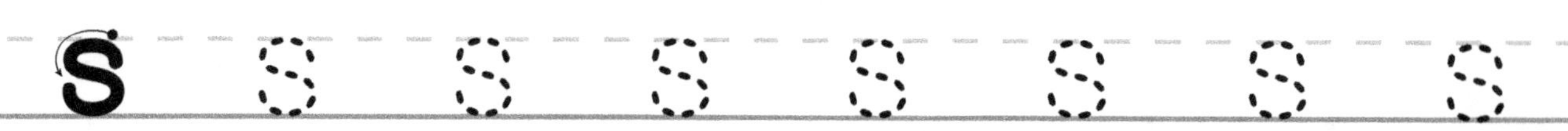

PRACTICE WORKSHEET

S S S S S S S S

s s s s s s s s

S S S S S S S S

s s s s s s s s

T is for Turkey

Trace the letters with a pencil. Then practice writing the letters on the lines

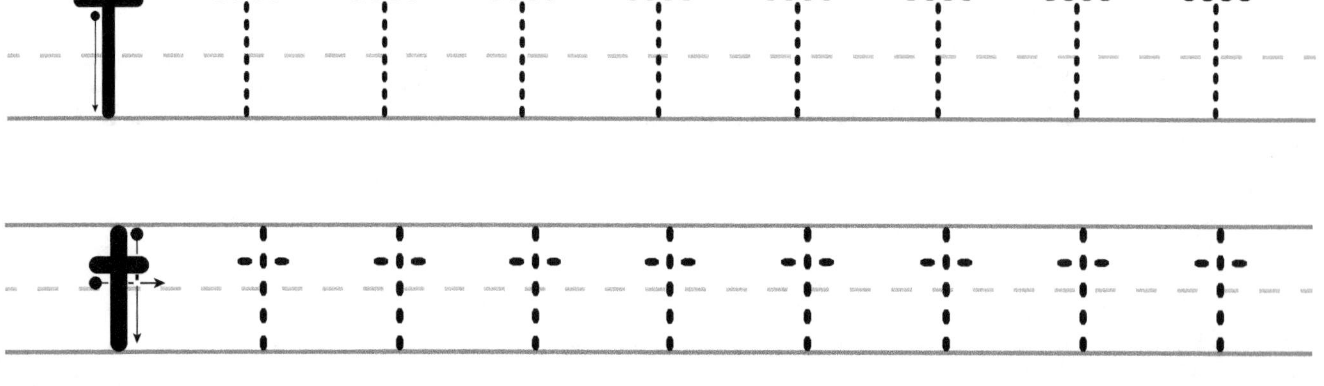

PRACTICE WORKSHEET

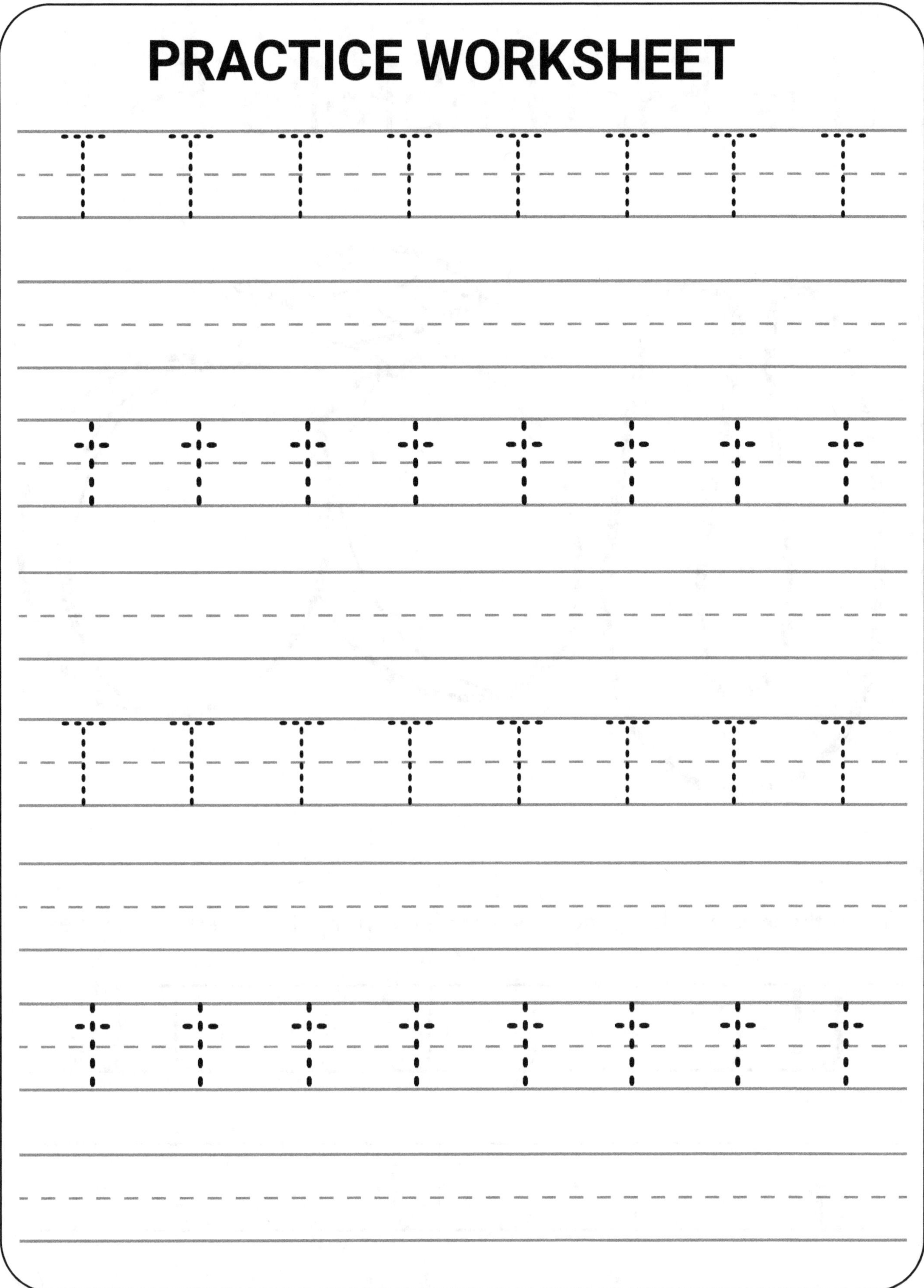

U is For Umbrella Fruit

Trace the letters with a pencil. Then practice writing the letters on the lines

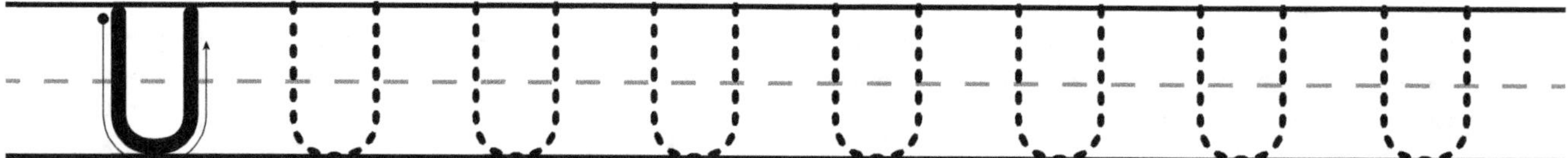

PRACTICE WORKSHEET

U U U U U U U U

u u u u u u u u

U U U U U U U U

u u u u u u u u

V is For Vanilla

Trace the letters with a pencil. Then practice writing the letters on the lines

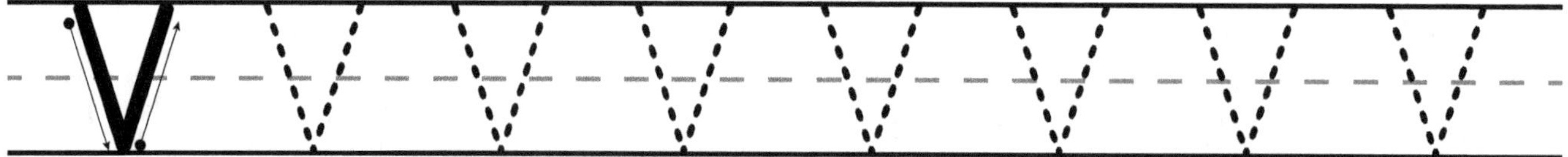

PRACTICE WORKSHEET

W is for Waffle

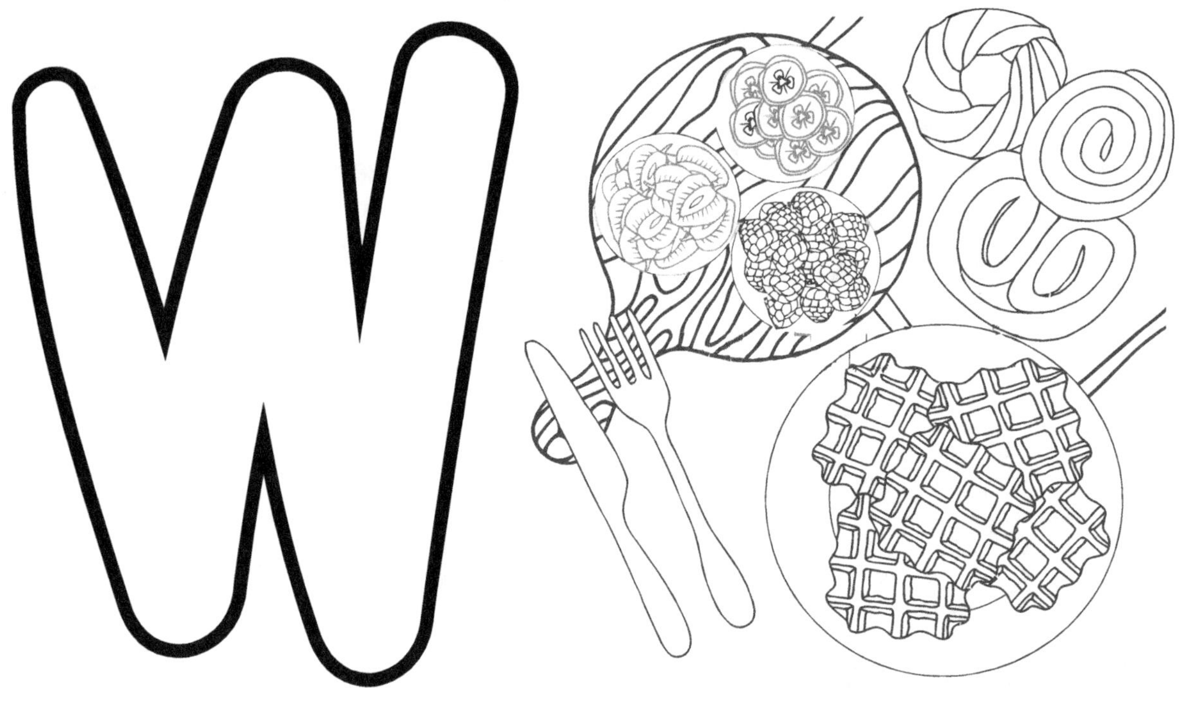

Trace the letters with a pencil. Then practice writing the letters on the lines

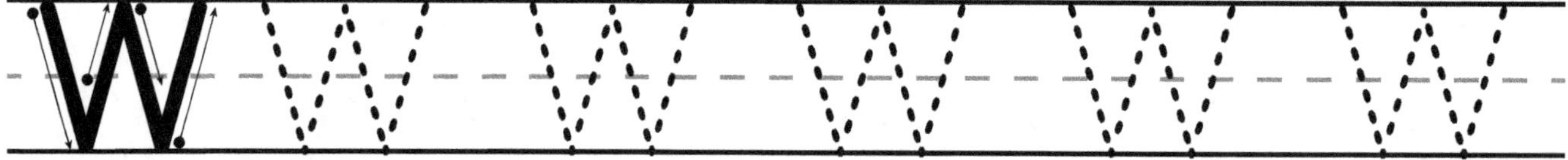

PRACTICE WORKSHEET

1

X is for X-ray

X

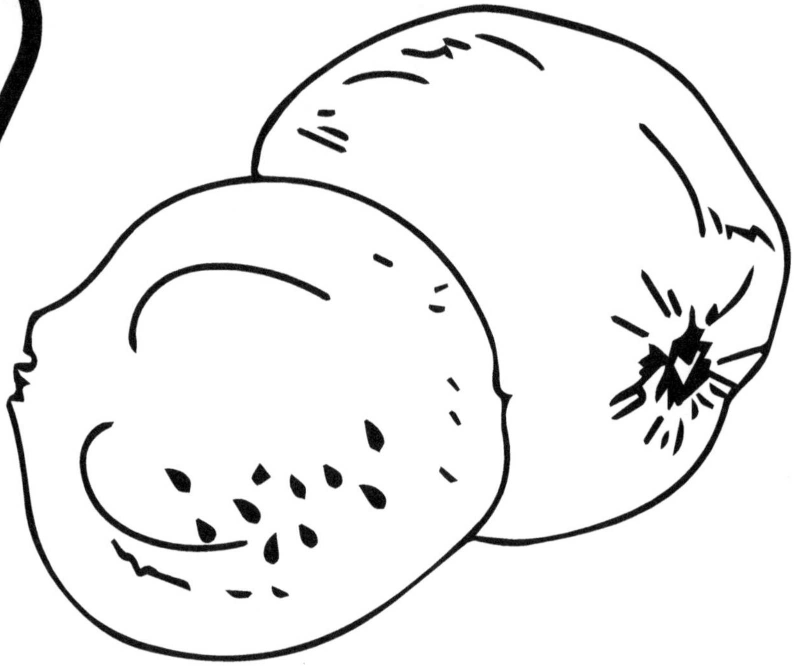

Trace the letters with a pencil. Then practice writing the letters on the lines

X X X X X X X X

x x x x x x x x

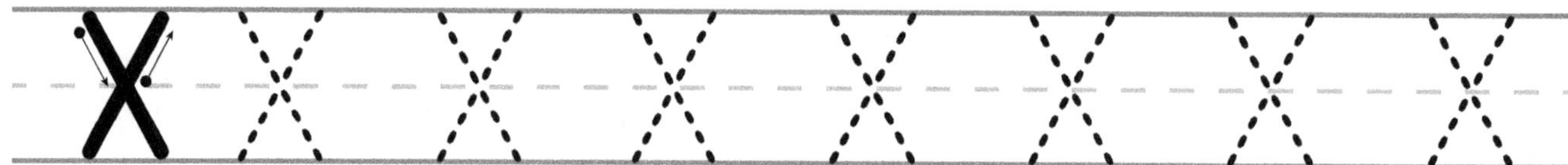

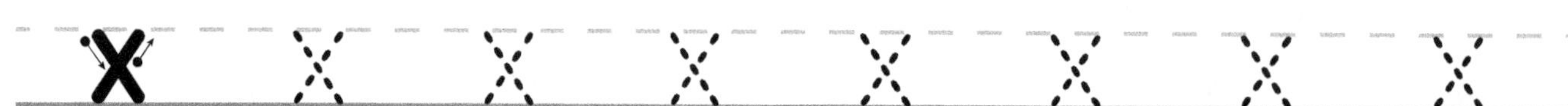

PRACTICE WORKSHEET

X X X X X X X X

x x x x x x x x

X X X X X X X X

x x x x x x x x

Y is for Yam

Trace the letters with a pencil. Then practice writing the letters on the lines

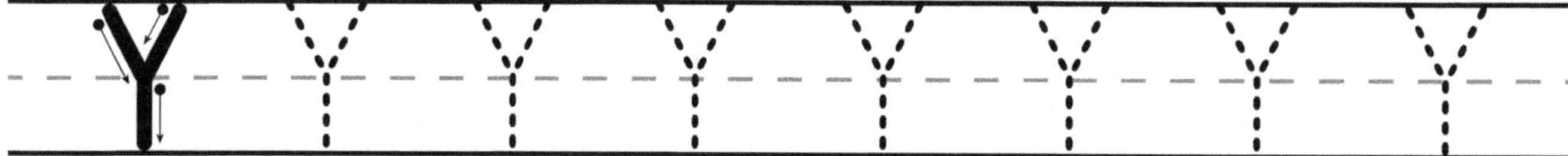

PRACTICE WORKSHEET

Y Y Y Y Y Y Y Y

y y y y y y y y

Y Y Y Y Y Y Y Y

y y y y y y y y

Z is for Zucchini

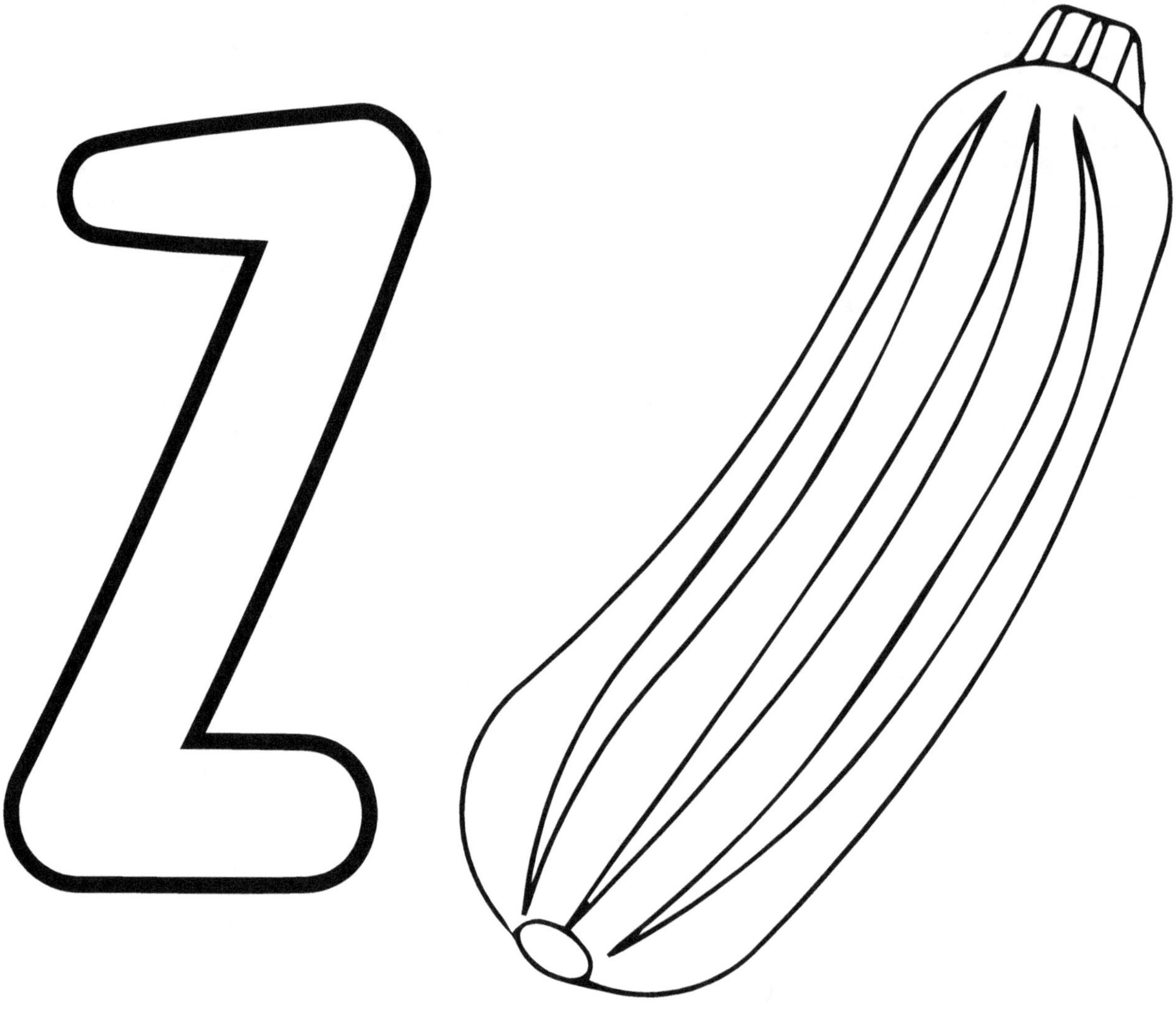

Trace the letters with a pencil. Then practice writing the letters on the lines

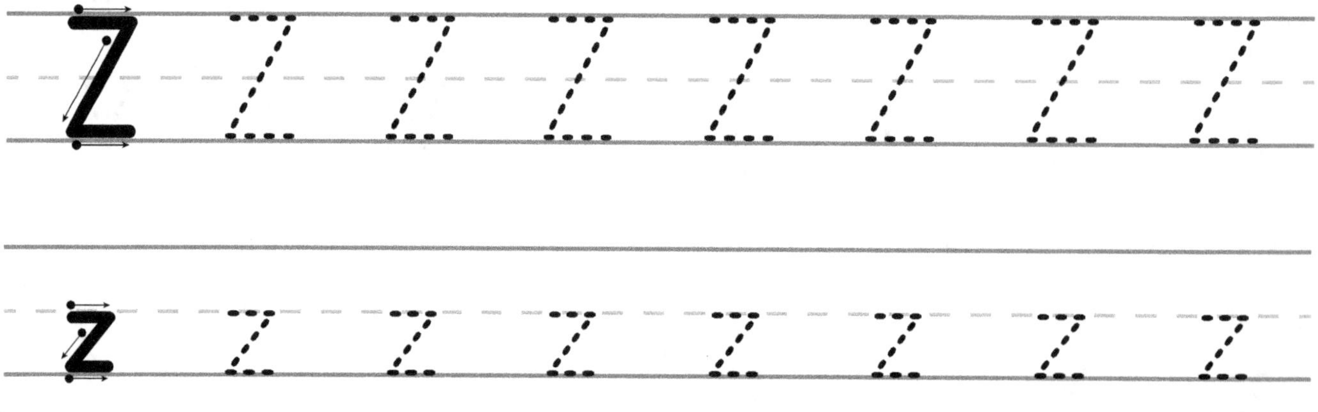

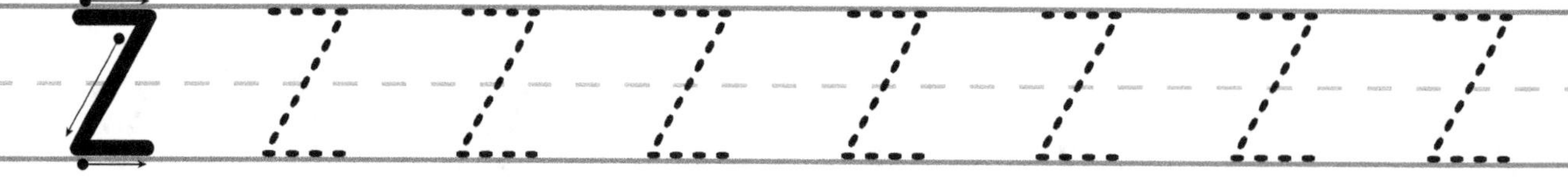

PRACTICE WORKSHEET

www.ingramcontent.com/pod-product-compliance
Lightning Source LLC
LaVergne TN
LVHW080558160826
845677LV00010B/1893

* 9 7 9 8 4 1 9 4 4 8 1 7 9 *